The Only Cohabitation Agreement Guide You'll Ever Need

A Canadian Lawyer Explains All

Jeffrey A Behrendt, BA, JD, LLM

CONTENTS

INTRODUCTION – The Only Cohabitation Agreement Guide You'll Ever Need

    Who is Jeffrey Behrendt?

    What is a Cohabitation Agreement?

    Why Get A Cohabitation Agreement?

    What should I put in my Cohabitation Agreement?

Chapter 1: VALIDITY

    Independent Legal Advice

    One Lawyer for Each of You

    Fairness

    Financial Disclosure

    Subject Matter

    Fault

    Timing

Formalities

Marriage

Chapter 2: COMMON LAW RELATIONSHIPS

What is Cohabitation?

Are We Cohabiting?

What if My Partner is or I am Still Married to Someone Else?

How long do we have to be Living Together to be Common Law?

We've lived together a really long time – are we married?

CHAPTER 3: CUSTODY AND ACCESS

What is the Law regarding Custody and Access?

Custody and Access in a Cohabitation Agreement

Options for Custody and Access

Chapter 4: CHILD SUPPORT

What is Child Support?

What is the Law regarding Child Support?

Child Support and a New Relationship

Child Support in a Cohabitation Agreement

Step-Parents and Child Support

StepParents and Cohabitation Agreements

Chapter 5: SPOUSAL SUPPORT

What is Spousal Support (also known as Alimony, Maintenance, Spousal Maintenance)?

Do Common Law Partners Pay Spousal Support?

Determining Spousal Support

Spousal Support and a New Relationship

Immigration and Spousal Support

Spousal Support in a Cohabitation Agreement

    Spousal Support Options

Chapter 6: PROPERTY DIVISION

    What is Property?

    What is the Law regarding Division of Property?

    Unjust Enrichment

    Joint Family Venture

    Quantum Meruit

    Constructive Trust

    Property Division in a Cohabitation Agreement

    Property Division Options

Chapter 7: MATRIMONIAL HOME

    What is the Law regarding Matrimonial Homes?

    Matrimonial Home Rights

    Matrimonial Homes in a Cohabitation Agreement

    Matrimonial Home Options

Chapter 8: ESTATES

    Estates and Cohabitation

    What is the Law regarding Estates?

    But wait...

    There's more...

    Estates in a Cohabitation Agreement

    Estate Law Options

Chapter 9: JURISDICTIONAL ISSUES

    What is the Law regarding Jurisdiction?

    Jurisdiction in a Cohabitation Agreement

CONCLUSION

MORE INFORMATION

In addition to authoring *The Only Cohabitation Agreement Guide You'll Ever Need*, Jeffrey Behrendt, B.A., J.D., LL.M. produces and hosts Canada's leading website about Cohabitation Agreements. You can learn more about Jeff, and obtain free supplemental materials, at CohabitationAgreement.ca.

INTRODUCTION – The Only Cohabitation Agreement Guide You'll Ever Need

In this book, I've taken my experience creating and negotiating cohabitation agreements, since my call to the bar over 16 years ago, and written a complete guide for Canadian couples thinking about entering into a cohabitation agreement.

This brief, easy-to-read book takes you through every step of the process without any legalese. I give you a solid background about the complexities of how family and estate law works for unmarried couples who are cohabiting, what you can do with a cohabitation agreement to change this, and how the process works.

Inside this complete guide you will discover:

- How spousal support and property division work for common law couples
- What makes a valid cohabitation agreement
- How custody, access, and child support are affected by cohabitation agreements
- What your cohabitation agreement can say about spousal support
- How property can be divided in a cohabitation agreement
- Cohabitation agreements and estate planning

And much more.

Each chapter guides you through the various legal issues of a cohabitation agreement. Common questions I get from my clients are answered and the most common options couples choose when agreeing to a cohabitation agreement are laid out.

You can pay a lawyer hundreds or even thousands of dollars in legal fees to learn this information and help you decide what would work best for you in a cohabitation agreement. Or, you can read this complete guide and get all your questions answered, in easy-to-understand language.

Who is Jeffrey Behrendt?

This is a practical book about cohabitation agreements. Will it help you? Is it accurate? Who the heck am I to author it?

I am a lawyer practising family and estates law in Ottawa, Ontario. I was called to the bar in 2000, and run my own law firm.

Since I was called to the bar, I've noticed a substantial increase in the number of people inquiring about, and entering into, cohabitation agreements to the point where cohabitation agreements and prenuptial agreements have become a substantial part of my legal practice.

People come to me nervous and confused, and even embarrassed about their desire to enter into a cohabitation agreement. They have many questions, and the law applying to common law couples is not a simple matter.

If you are in that situation, then you are not alone. This book is here to provide you with a complete guide to cohabitation agreements in Canada, and how to set one up. It follows on the heels of my bestselling book: *Prenup Essentials – What Canadians Need to Know.*

In law school, they teach you to "think like a lawyer" and to speak "legalese." Over the years, through my activities such as instructing paralegal students, publishing articles in newspapers and magazines, and radio and television interviews, I have worked hard to break down complex legal concepts so that they are easy to understand. While I can't eliminate all legalese from a book about the law, you can rest assured that everything in this book is as simple and straightforward as it can be.

I attended the University of Waterloo in Waterloo, Ontario on both a Descartes Scholarship and a Canada Scholarship. In 1993, I graduated on the Dean's Honour's List with a Bachelor of Arts Degree in Economics. In 1996, I graduated with a Juris Doctor Degree from the University of Toronto Faculty of Law in Toronto. While in law school, I was an Associate Editor of the University of Toronto Law Review. I continued my education in England, graduating with Merit in 1998 with a Master of Laws Degree from King's College London.

I've done two judicial clerkships: one at the Commonwealth Court of Pennsylvania in Philadelphia, Pennsylvania and one at the Third Circuit Court of Appeals in Pittsburgh, Pennsylvania.

I live in Ottawa, with my son Emet.

You can contact me through my website CohabitationAgreement.ca, Canada's leading website dealing with cohabitation agreements.

What is a Cohabitation Agreement?

A cohabitation agreement is an agreement that sets out what happens financially when your relationship ends. Your relationship will always end – either by separation or eventually death. I know… it is not pleasant to think about!

Whether you specifically enter into a cohabitation agreement or not, the fact is that you are bound by one, namely the rules set out in the family law statute and the estates law statute of your province or territory, as well as many previous decisions made by judges (known as "case law") deciding what the rights of cohabiting couples are.

Note that in Saskatchewan cohabitation agreements are known as interspousal contracts.

Additionally, often lawyers refer to cohabitation agreements, prenuptial agreements, separation agreements, and paternity agreements generically as domestic contracts.

Why Get A Cohabitation Agreement?

Unlike for married couples, even if you are happy with the rules set out by the legislature and courts, it still makes sense to enter into a cohabitation agreement. There are several good reasons for this.

First, the rules for property division for unmarried couples are very vague in many provinces and territories. When a married couple separates, a lawyer can look at their financial situation and explain how their property will be divided between them. While there are rules for property division for unmarried couples, in many provinces and territories there is a lot of greyness in those rules, and so it is difficult even for a lawyer to predict how property will be divided. That makes these sorts of cases difficult to settle, as it makes it worthwhile to take your chances in court to see if you will get a judge favourable to your position.

Additionally, common law property division cases can be a lot of work to prove in court, leading to a large legal bill, regardless of outcome. So, in short, uncertain outcome plus a complicated case makes property division for unmarried couples in most provinces and territories a mess. A cohabitation agreement can make the situation clear, allowing you and your partner to avoid this legal mess.

Second, the law relating to common law couples is changing over time. While you may be happy with the way the law treats unmarried couples now, over time the law is changing. As time goes on, common law couples are treated more and more like married couples, either through changes in legislation, or through judges making it easier for people to get a result similar to that of a married couple.

This may not be what you want, and may in fact be one reason why you are cohabiting rather than getting married. The relevant law that will apply to your situation is the law when your relationship ends, not the law as it stood when your relationship began. A cohabitation agreement helps you avoid future, unpredictable changes in family and estate law.

Third, similar to the situation with the law changing over time, you may move to a different province during your relationship. Each province and territory treats common law couples very differently, and you may lose or gain substantial family law and estate rights, simply because your employer transferred you or your partner to a different office across the country.

Fourth, a cohabitation agreement can prove… cohabitation. You may think that is strange, but unlike a marriage, where people get married on a particular day, cohabitation is often a gradual process, with couples spending more and more time together.

Couples can disagree when cohabitation started. For instance, some rights of unmarried couples may arise after three years of cohabitation. One partner may genuinely believe that the couple has been living together for three years and one month, while the other party may genuinely believe that the couple has been living together for two years and eleven months. Alternatively, one party may claim that they did not have a common law relationship, but rather a landlord tenant relationship.

There may also be an estate law situation, where the family of the deceased person is arguing that you were not cohabiting with the deceased, or may not agree with you about the date you and your partner started living together. Again, a cohabitation agreement allows you to avoid all these issues.

Finally, in many provinces and territories, for estate law purposes, common law partners are strangers to each other in law. So, if one partner passes away without a will, the other partner may well get nothing. This may not be the result you and your partner want.

As well, in many provinces and territories, there is no obligation to provide for a common law partner in a will. This means a person can completely disinherit a partner, even if they have lived together in a happy relationship for many years. This may be a desired result in a situation where both partners have children from a previous relationship, but otherwise may not be desired. A cohabitation agreement can help ensure that upon one partner passing away, the other partner is treated fairly.

I know it is somewhat of a conflict of interest as I make a living preparing cohabitation agreements, but based on the above, I truly believe that it is in every unmarried couples' best interest to enter into a cohabitation agreement.

What should I put in my Cohabitation Agreement?

The simple answer is whatever you and your partner agree to, and believe is fair. However, that is not really all that helpful, is it? Some people know very clearly what they want, while others are unsure.

To complicate matters further, most people starting to live together are unaware of what family law and estate law rules govern their common law relationship, or believe those rules are unfair or do not properly reflect their priorities and values.

The idea behind each chapter of this book is as follows. First, I will inform you as to what the rules that govern common law relationships are. Next, I will explain to you whether a cohabitation agreement can change those rules, and how. Third, I will provide background so that you and your partner can decide what to put in your cohabitation agreement so that it reflects your priorities and values. Finally, I will go through the most common things I see clients include in their cohabitation agreements, and the reasons behind this.

Chapter 1: VALIDITY

The first thing most people want to know about cohabitation agreements is – are they valid? Yes, they are. Well then, why do you hear so many stories about cohabitation agreements being invalidated in court? Two reasons:

(1) Many of these stories are American. The legal situation there is quite different from here in Canada, where many provinces even have specific legislation dealing with cohabitation agreements.

(2) Not using a lawyer. I know you might think I am biased because I am a lawyer, but I am a big proponent of self-help in the family law area. However, the law regarding cohabitation agreements is an area of law that is too hazardous to go forward without a lawyer even if you and your partner want a "simple" agreement. That is why this book does not include any templates for you to prepare your own agreement.

In short: if both you and your partner have a lawyer, and both of your lawyers sign off on the agreement, then your cohabitation agreement is almost certain to be valid.

Independent Legal Advice

When entering into a cohabitation agreement, it is important to retain a lawyer to provide you with what is known as "independent legal advice." The lawyer will go through the agreement with you, explain what each of the terms means, ensure that you understand them, ensure that you understand how your family law and estate law rights are impacted by your cohabitation agreement, answer any questions you have, and make recommendations about any changes that should be made to the agreement.

This independent legal advice offers protection against three typical grounds of attack on a cohabitation agreement:

(1) "**I didn't understand the agreement**." Your partner may be an educated person with a Master's or even a Ph.D., but if you separate and he or she is not happy with the cohabitation agreement, they are going to claim that they did not understand the agreement. This is a difficult claim to dispute – a cohabitation agreement is full of legalese that is difficult to understand unless you are a lawyer. However, if your partner consulted a lawyer beforehand, then the lawyer has explained the agreement to him or her, and they cannot attack the cohabitation agreement on this ground.

(2) "**I didn't understand my legal rights**." You may draft your cohabitation agreement in the plainest English that anyone can understand. However, your partner can still attack the cohabitation agreement on the ground that he or she did not understand their legal rights. For instance, the cohabitation agreement may say spousal support is 10% of the payor's income – this is clear and easy to understand. However, if your partner is not aware of the Spousal Support Advisory Guidelines, and the amount of spousal support they are entitled to pursuant to the Guidelines, then their attack on the agreement will be difficult to defend. In this example, by consulting a lawyer, your partner would have been advised about how spousal support works, and what their entitlement to spousal support would be without

the cohabitation agreement.

(3) "**I was pressured into signing the agreement**." This becomes a he-said, she-said type of situation where one partner claims the agreement was entered into voluntarily and the other one claims that he or she was pressured into signing it. Again, using a lawyer prevents such a claim. A lawyer will ask their client whether they are being pressured into signing an agreement, and will sign a certificate stating that there was no such pressure if that is the case.

One Lawyer for Each of You

It would be really efficient if one lawyer could represent both you and your partner, especially if both of you agree on what should go into your cohabitation agreement. However, the "independent" part of the independent legal advice is important – a lawyer is only permitted to represent one side of the agreement, even if both of you agree on everything. So you will each need a separate lawyer.

Typically, one party's lawyer prepares the agreement, then the other party's lawyer reviews it and suggests changes.

Your partner does not want a lawyer? That may just be a polite way of sabotaging the cohabitation agreement. They are essentially trying to leave open at least three grounds on which to attack the cohabitation agreement in the future.

If your partner cannot afford a lawyer, you are free to pay for the lawyer on their behalf. Even though you are paying the lawyer, the lawyer will only represent your partner. This is a worthwhile investment to ensure that your cohabitation agreement is valid.

Legal fees are expensive, and ideally you and your partner understand the basics of the legal framework governing cohabitation agreements. The information in this book is designed to help you do just that. As well, it is helpful if you and your partner agree about what you want your cohabitation agreement to accomplish prior to consulting with a lawyer, as it can get quite expensive to negotiate a cohabitation agreement through lawyers.

Fairness

A cohabitation agreement does not have to be "fair." However, the reality is it cannot be too one-sided, otherwise a court will invalidate it.

The court's test in Ontario and most other provinces and territories is "unconscionability." If an agreement is unconscionable – that is, it shocks the court's conscience, then a court will invalidate it. In other words, if your cohabitation agreement gives you a good deal, then it is fine. If it gives you more than just a good deal – let's call it too good a deal – then it may not be upheld in court.

In British Columbia, the standard is whether the cohabitation agreement is significantly unfair. This is a new standard that was just introduced in 2013, and there is not yet a lot of case law about this in relation to cohabitation agreements. However, it is likely that this standard is a bit lower than that of unconscionability.

Keep in mind that what is fair can vary dramatically depending on the length of your relationship. What is fair in a two-year relationship may be very different from what is fair in a twenty-year relationship. Ideally your cohabitation agreement is flexible enough to deal with both the short run and the long run.

Regardless of the standard, you want to protect your interests, but you do not want to take advantage of your partner, nor leave them in financial trouble, should your relationship end. If you take advantage of your partner, the court will intervene and set aside your cohabitation agreement.

Financial Disclosure

For a cohabitation agreement to be valid, there must be full financial disclosure. The idea is that you and your partner cannot enter into an agreement dealing with your finances, unless you are aware of the complete financial picture of your partner.

You will need to disclose to your partner your income from all sources, all of your assets and their values, and all of your liabilities and their amounts. This information is then put into a financial statement that becomes part of the cohabitation agreement.

It is also a good idea to exchange financial disclosure with your partner – that is, exchange documents supporting the figures in your financial statement. This is in case the accuracy of your financial statement is ever challenged in an attempt to invalidate the cohabitation agreement. So, you want to gather up your notices of assessment for the previous three years, a recent pay stub, and bank statements for all of your bank accounts, RRSPs, TFSA, credit cards, lines of credit, and so on. Your partner should do the same, and copies of these documents are exchanged to ensure the accuracy of your financial statement.

For some assets it is not possible to state a precise value – for instance, the value of your home or car. In these circumstances, an estimate is normally sufficient.

If you own a business, it is usually not necessary to get a formal business appraisal done, but in addition to the documents listed above, you will want to exchange your business' financial statements, tax returns, and notices of assessment for the last three years.

Pensions are a tricky asset and often have a different value for family law purposes than the pension plan uses. Again, it is normally not necessary to have the pension formally valued by an actuary; it is normally sufficient just to disclose its existence.

Subject Matter

There are certain things that one is not permitted to deal with in a cohabitation agreement; these are covered under the various subject-matter headings of this book. In short, most cohabitation agreements deal with property division and possibly spousal support; clauses dealing with children and child support are usually not valid.

Fault

I often get requests that there be clauses like "if someone commits adultery, then they must pay a penalty of …" Clauses dealing with fault are not likely to be enforced. In Canada, all financial issues relating to separation, such as support and property division, are no fault. This means that they are based solely on economic considerations and not who is at fault in the breakdown of the relationship. The idea is that the breakdown of a relationship is complex and it is normally both parties' fault that a relationship has failed. Also, realistically, a judge does not want to hear all the gory details about who did what to whom in figuring out how to divide a couple's property.

Timing

Timing is a complex issue. In short, the earlier you can enter into a cohabitation agreement, the better. Ideally, you would enter into your cohabitation agreement prior to moving in together.

That being said, you can enter into a cohabitation agreement at any time during your relationship – even if you have been living together for many years already. However, the longer you wait, the more complicated the legal situation is, as often legal rights vest over time. Entering into a cohabitation agreement a few weeks or months after you start living together is quite a different situation than entering into one years later.

Formalities
There are a few other formalities that are necessary for a cohabitation agreement to be valid. The first is that it must be in writing. So, no matter what your partner promises you, if it is not in your written cohabitation agreement, it is not enforceable in court.

A cohabitation agreement must be signed and witnessed. The witness can be any adult of sound mind, so a friend, family member, or colleague can be a witness. The witness does not need to read the agreement; they are just confirming that they saw you sign the agreement. A cohabitation agreement does not get notarized.

It is a good idea for each party to initial every page of the agreement; this is to prevent pages from being switched out for new pages.

Marriage
What happens to your cohabitation agreement when you get married? It automatically becomes a prenuptial agreement and continues in effect. That being said, it is a good idea for

you and your partner to review the agreement before you get married to ensure that it still accurately reflects your values and financial situation.

Chapter 2: COMMON LAW RELATIONSHIPS

What is Cohabitation?

This is the threshold question – you will only need a cohabitation agreement if you are cohabiting or going to be cohabiting. In non-legal terms, if you consider yourself living in a marriage-like relationship, and you have lived together for the length of time required by law, then you are in a common law relationship, whether you are in a straight or same sex relationship.

Are We Cohabiting?

The reality is that life is not always simple and there are a wide variety of types of common law relationships. To determine whether you are common law, courts look at the following factors:

1. Shelter – did you and your partner live together;

2. Sexual and Personal Behaviour;

3. Services – did you and your partner help each other the way a traditional family would;

4. Social – did you and your partner portray yourselves as a couple;

5. Societal – how did the community view your relationship;

6. Economic Support – was one partner supporting the other financially, or were your finances combined?; and

7. Children – did you interact parentally with each other's children?

I do not want to get overly technical in this book. However, it is useful to see how courts have applied these factors in cases.

Here is a summary of some important cases where cohabitation was found to exist:

(a) Hazlewood v. Kent, [2000] O.J. No. 5263 (Ont. Fam. Ct.)

The parties were the parents of two children. The father worked in one community but spent his weekends at the mother's residence. The father had a room at the mother's residence in which he kept things of a personal nature. The mother cleaned the father's room. The parties had discussed marriage and had jointly met with a financial planner. The father had named the mother on an application for extended health benefits through his employment. The parties spent their weekends together sharing common activities as a family. The father had given his coworkers the telephone number of the mother in the event that he needed to be called on weekends. The parties had considered marriage.

(b) Thauvette v. Malyon, [1996] O.J. No. 1356 (Ont. Gen. Div.)

The parties began an affair while both were living with other partners, seeing each other 2-3 times each week. After three years of the affair, Thauvette left her spouse and moved into a home owned by Malyon and for which Malyon continued to pay all of the expenses. A year later Malyon also left his spouse but the parties chose to maintain separate residences to keep the children apart and to facilitate Malyon's access to his children. When Thauvette moved out of the home provided for her by Malyon, Malyon helped her with the purchase price of another residence with an advance of $30,000. Thauvette helped Malyon on a regular basis with his farming operation, working with the animals and doing domestic chores. They spend 4-5 nights each week together during this period of their relationship.

(c) McEachem v. Fry Estate, [1993] O.J. No. 1731 (Ont. Gen. Div.)

Following the death of their respective spouses the parties commenced a relationship that lasted for 15 years until the death of Mr. Fry. While they maintained separate residences and pursued some of their own interests, they spent the bulk of their free time together including at least two nights each week at the other's residence. They socialized as a couple in public. They took annual vacations together each year. Ms McEachern did domestic chores at his house and he paid for maintenance items at her house. He provided clothes for her costing at least $2500 annually. He bought her a fur coat. He provided for her in his will. They were known as a couple within the community and were faithful to one another. They celebrated their "anniversary" each year.

Here are some cases where cohabitation was found not to exist:

(a) Obringer v. Kennedy Estate (1996), 16 E.T.R. (2d) 27 (Ont. Gen. Div.)

The parties had a twenty year, intimate, exclusive relationship, which included sexual relations, holidays together, gift exchanges, personal services and joint friends and acquaintances. Cohabitation was not found, however, as there was no common residence and they were financially independent of one another.

(b) Nowell v. Town Estate 1994 CanLII 7285 (ON SC), (1994), 5 R.F.L. (4th) 353 (Ont. Gen. Div.)

The parties had a 24-year affair, maintaining separate residences. Town was married and living with his wife at the time and Nowell knew of her existence. The parties were together most weekends at his farm/work studio and did some work together. They maintained separate residences.

What if My Partner is or I am Still Married to Someone Else?

Oftentimes, people separate and start a new relationship with a new partner without getting a divorce from their previous partner first. However, the fact that one or both partners is still legally married to a third party does not affect common law rights, and you should still consider entering into a cohabitation agreement in these circumstances.

How long do we have to be Living Together to be Common Law?

The answer to this question is going to be different for every particular right or obligation – e.g. it will be different for income taxes, Canada Pension Plan, spousal support, and property division. So, you could be considered common law for one purpose, but not for another. Additionally, it will also differ for some rights or obligations from province to province, and as well as if you and your partner have children together. As we go through this book, we will discuss all the relevant time periods for family and estate law purposes.

But in a way, this question does not matter for purposes of obtaining a cohabitation agreement. It is best if you get a cohabitation agreement as soon as you start living together (or even beforehand), rather than waiting until you are considered common law.

We've lived together a really long time – are we married?

No. There is no such thing as common law marriage in Canada. No matter how long you live together, the law will not consider you married.

CHAPTER 3: CUSTODY AND ACCESS

What is Custody and Access?

Custody and access relate to children. Custody is the right to make the important decisions in your child's life, such as health care decisions, educational decisions, and religious decisions. Access is the right to spend time with your child – it is essentially the schedule the children follow as to which parent's home they reside in.

What is the Law regarding Custody and Access?

Custody and access are always decided in a child's best interests. This is a pretty malleable standard that can mean different things to different people. Under section 24(2) of Ontario's Children's Law Reform Act, the following factors are considered:

(a) the love, affection and emotional ties between the child and,
(i) each person entitled to or claiming custody of or access to the child,
(ii) other members of the child's family who reside with the child, and
(iii) persons involved in the child's care and upbringing;
(b) the child's views and preferences, if they can reasonably be ascertained;
(c) the length of time the child has lived in a stable home environment;
(d) the ability and willingness of each person applying for custody of the child to provide the child with guidance and education, the necessaries of life and any special needs of the child;
(e) the plan proposed by each person applying for custody of or access to the child for the child's care and upbringing;
(f) the permanence and stability of the family unit with which it is proposed that the child will live;
(g) the ability of each person applying for custody of or access to the child to act as a parent; and
(h) the relationship by blood or through an adoption order between the child and each person who is a party to the application.

Each province and territory has their own legislation, but considerations are pretty much the same everywhere.

Custody and Access in a Cohabitation Agreement

The law is clear that a cohabitation agreement cannot deal with custody of, and access to, children. The idea behind this is that parents cannot know in advance what is in their children's best interests.

There are some exceptions to this, namely that one is permitted to "direct the education and moral training of their children" in a cohabitation agreement.

Given the limited scope for dealing with custody and access in a cohabitation agreement, people don't normally deal with this. However, there are some types of clauses you can put in that deal with children.

Options for Custody and Access

Here are some options you can consider:

OPTION: Cultural heritage
You can put in your cohabitation agreement that you and partner intend to educate your children about a particular cultural heritage (or even language). Or you can put in that your children will have a Bar/Bat Mitzvah or similar milestone.

OPTION: Private school
Your cohabitation agreement can state that it is your intention to send your children to a private school (obviously, depending on finances and your children meeting the school's admission criteria). Alternatively, you can agree to a particular type of school: for instance, a French-language school or a Catholic school.

OPTION: Post-secondary education
Your cohabitation agreement can state that you intend to send your children to college or university (again, depending on your finances and your children's abilities).

OPTION: No permanent removal from jurisdiction
Where parents are from different places, you may want to make it clear that no child will be permanently removed from the municipality in which you and your partner reside without the written consent of the other parent.

Chapter 4: CHILD SUPPORT

What is Child Support?

If you and your child's other parent do not live together, there is an automatic obligation for one parent to pay the other child support. If a child resides primarily with one parent, the other parent will be the one to pay child support. Even if a child resides equally with both parents, the higher-income parent will normally pay child support to the lower-income parent. These payments are made to help cover the expenses involved in raising the children.

What is the Law regarding Child Support?

The amount of child support one is required to pay is based on tables that are part of the Child Support Guidelines. You can find a handy online calculator at:
http://www.justice.gc.ca/eng/fl-df/child-enfant/look-rech.asp

So, someone in Ontario earning $75,000 per year with two children is required to pay $1,105 per month in child support. Note that this amount is NOT tax deductible – so it is paid in after tax dollars.

In addition to the table amount of child support, a parent is expected to contribute to what are known as special or extraordinary expenses. Examples of this are orthodontist expenses, private school tuition, before and after school care fees, costs of expensive extracurricular activities, and so on. These expenses are shared in proportion to the parents' income. So, if you are earning $75,000 per year, and the other parent is earning $25,000 per year, in addition to the table amount of child support, you are required to pay 75% of all your children's special or extraordinary expenses.

Child Support and a New Relationship

One question I often get asked is will the amount of child support I pay go up because I am entering into a new relationship? The answer is no (except in unusual circumstances, such as your child support having been reduced due to undue hardship).

Child Support in a Cohabitation Agreement

The main principle to keep in mind regarding child support is that a court is free to disregard any provision in a cohabitation agreement relating to child support. In short, you can put whatever you want about child support into a cohabitation agreement, but it is almost certain that it will not be enforceable in court. The idea behind this is that child support is the right of the child, and the child is not a party to the cohabitation agreement.

This principle makes a lot of sense in a traditional situation where a young couple is just starting out in life and plan to have children in the future. However, a large percentage of people entering into cohabitation agreements are entering into a second or subsequent relationship, and already have children from a previous relationship. What most people do not realize is that <u>step-parents can be liable for child support</u>. This is true even if the biological parent is paying child support. So, for instance, a mother can obtain child support from both the biological father, and a step-father.

Step-Parents and Child Support

The test to determine whether a stepparent must pay child support is whether the stepparent has stood "in the place of a parent for the child" or as lawyers often say "in loco parentis." Generally, if you have lived with a child for any substantial amount of time, you may well have a liability for child support.

However, if you had a more transient relationship, then you may not need to pay child support.

Even if your relationship with the stepchildren is strained, has broken off, or was never very strong, or even if it was the reason for you breaking up with your partner, you may well be found to have acted in loco parentis to the children. This is particularly so if you financially supported the children beforehand, even in an indirect way such as making mortgage payments on the home that the children lived in.

The amount of child support a step-parent is required to pay is at the court's discretion — there are no tables for this, as in the ordinary child support situation. One commonly applied "rule of thumb" is to calculate how much the stepparent would be required to pay under the Child Support Guidelines, then deduct from that the amount of child support that the biological parent is paying.

If the biological parent is not paying anything (for instance, the biological parent is unemployed, ill, or cannot be located), then the stepparent may be responsible for paying the full table amount of child support. A stepparent, then, may be required to pay any amount ranging from a token top-up amount to the full amount called for by the Child Support Guidelines.

StepParents and Cohabitation Agreements

I often get asked by people to put provisions in their cohabitation agreements that state that they will not have any responsibility to pay child support for their stepchildren. As with child support in the traditional situation, the court is free to disregard such provisions. Again, child support is the right of the stepchildren, and the stepchildren are not a party to the cohabitation agreement.

It can still make sense for stepparents to include these provisions in their cohabitation agreements. It does offer some evidence that the stepparent did not intend to act in loco parentis to the stepchildren.

As well, even if the provision is not legally binding, it may well be morally persuasive. A lot of people are true to their word, even if a court won't force them to be. So, feel free to include such provisions in your agreement. However, just be aware that if push comes to shove, you may still end up paying child support, regardless of what your cohabitation agreement says.

Chapter 5: SPOUSAL SUPPORT

What is Spousal Support (also known as Alimony, Maintenance, Spousal Maintenance)?

When a couple separates, often the higher income earning partner will end up paying spousal support to the lower income earning partner. This is known as spousal support. It is awarded to compensate partners for the roles they played during the relationship, and any disadvantages they suffer as a result of the relationship ending.

Do Common Law Partners Pay Spousal Support?

In short, yes, after a period of time that varies from province to province, and often is different if the couple has children. Generally, the period of cohabitation must be continuous. Here are the specifics:

Ontario

Spousal support is payable if you and your partner have cohabited for three years, or if you and your partner live in a relationship of permanence and have a child together.

British Columbia

Spousal support is payable if you and your partner have lived together in a marriage-like relationship for at least two years, or you lived in a marriage-like relationship for less than two years and have a child together.

Alberta

Spousal support is payable if you and your partner have lived together in a relationship of interdependence for three years, or if you and your partner have lived together in a relationship of interdependence for less than three years, but the relationship is of some permanence, and there is a child of the relationship, or if you and your partner enter into an Adult Interdependent Partner Agreement.

Saskatchewan
Spousal support is payable if you and your partner have cohabited continuously for a period of not less than two years, or cohabited in a relationship of some permanence if you and your partner are parents of a child.

Manitoba
Spousal support is payable if you and your partner have lived together in a conjugal relationship for three years, or if you and your partner have lived in a conjugal relationship for one year and are raising a child together, or if you and your partner have registered your relationship under the Vital Statistics Act.

Nova Scotia
Spousal support is payable if you and your partner have cohabited for two years, or if you and your partner have registered your relationship by filing a domestic partners declaration under the Vital Statistics Act.

New Brunswick
Spousal support is payable if you and your partner have cohabited for three years, or if you and your partner have cohabited for one year and had a child.

Newfoundland and Labrador
Spousal support is payable if you and your partner have cohabited in a conjugal relationship outside of marriage for a period of at least two years, or for a period of at least one year, where you and your partner are, together, the parents of a child (known as partner support in Newfoundland and Labrador).

Prince Edward Island
Spousal support is payable if you and your partner have cohabited in a conjugal relationship continuously for a period of at least three years, or if you and your partner cohabited in a conjugal relationship and together are the parents of a child.

Northwest Territories
Spousal support is payable if you and your partner have lived in a marriage-like relationship for two years or more, of if you and your partner have lived in a marriage-like relationship for less than two years and have a child together.

Yukon
Spousal support is payable if you and your partner have lived in a relationship of some permanence.

Nunavut
Spousal support is payable if you and your partner have lived in a conjugal relationship for a period of at least two years, or if you and your partner have lived in a relationship of some permanence and are together the parents of a child.

Note also that under many provincial acts, the deadlines for applying for spousal support are different for common law couples than they are for married couples (as short as three months from the date of separation in Yukon).

Determining Spousal Support

There are two steps in determining spousal support. The first step is determining whether there is an entitlement to spousal support. If there is an entitlement to spousal support, the next step is determining the amount of spousal support.

Regarding entitlement, the types of things that create an entitlement to spousal support are choices, such as sacrificing your career to raise children, or to accommodate your partner's career, for instance by moving from city to city, making it difficult to progress in your career, actively working to promote your partner's career, for instance through regular business entertaining, and so on. However, the reality is that in most longer relationships, particularly where there is a large income differential between the partners, a court will find an entitlement to spousal support.

The amount of spousal support awarded is in the court's discretion. There are guidelines, known as the Spousal Support Advisory Guidelines. Unlike the Child Support Guidelines, these are advisory only; courts are not required to follow them. However, realistically, generally the courts do follow them unless there are really exceptional circumstances.

The Guidelines also provide a range of support, and usually the argument between partners is whether support should be paid at the high or low end of the range. A court will decide where in the range given by the Guidelines, based on a number of factors, such as your income, your partner's income, your health, your partner's health, the roles each of you played during the relationship, and so on.

Spousal support is tax deductible; so your actual out-of-pocket cost of paying spousal support is less than the amount you are paying.

You can find an online spousal support calculator prepared by a colleague of mine at:
https://www.mcgurk.ca/spousal-support-calculator/

If you play around with the calculator, you will note that spousal support payments are surprisingly high. For example, if you earn $100,000 and your partner is a stay-at-home parent with two children, you will pay child support of $1,416 per month, plus most of the children's special or extraordinary expenses, plus between $1,226 and $1,722 per month in spousal support. When you take taxes, CPP deductions, and EI deductions into account, you will only be left with a bit more than $40,000 per year after paying child support and the high range of spousal support.

The length of time spousal support is payable depends on whether there are children. The minimum length of time spousal support is payable is half the length of the relationship. So, if you were married for 10 years, spousal support would be payable for at least 5 years. If there are no children, spousal support generally ends no later than the number of years your relationship lasted. So, for a 10-year relationship, you would pay spousal support for up to 10 years.

For a relationship with children, spousal support could go even longer – until the children all finish their first post-secondary degree. What's more, a court is often loathe to predict when you will no longer need to pay spousal support, so for long-term relationships, spousal support will generally be indefinite. Indefinite means that the court does not set an end date – you will need to go back to court in the future to try to stop spousal support.

Spousal Support and a New Relationship

Will your new relationship effect the amount of spousal support you pay or receive? Quite possibly. At the very least, a new relationship by a spousal support payor or recipient will likely be grounds for review of spousal support. This question is too fact specific to know for sure in advance – you will realistically need to spend an hour or so with a lawyer reviewing the details of your situation.

If you are a spousal support recipient, there is no automatic presumption that just because you are moving in with someone, your spousal support will end or be reduced. However, you may have entered into a separation agreement that states this will happen. If that is not the case, it is going to depend on the reason you are receiving spousal support. If it is to compensate you for career losses during your relationship, then your new relationship is not likely to affect your spousal support, as those losses still require compensation. If you are receiving spousal support because of a need for support, your need for support may well be reduced because of your new relationship, in which case spousal support may well be reduced.

If you are a spousal support payor, it is possible that spousal support will go up if you marry. This will happen if the amount of spousal support you were paying was limited by your financial ability, but was not the amount needed by the support recipient or required to compensate for career losses.

Immigration and Spousal Support

If you plan on sponsoring your partner to live in Canada once you begin living together, you will sign an undertaking with the Federal government that you will support your partner for three years. This is an agreement between you and the government. As the government is not a party to your cohabitation agreement, nothing you put in your cohabitation agreement can override this.

Spousal Support in a Cohabitation Agreement

You can deal with spousal support in your cohabitation agreement, but you have to be careful what you put in your agreement. A court is going to scrutinize closely the spousal support provisions of a cohabitation agreement. As discussed in the chapter on validity, if a court finds them unconscionable (or grossly unfair in British Columbia), then the court will invalidate them. A stereotypical example of this would be if one partner is going to need social assistance due to the spousal support provisions in the cohabitation agreement. This would normally be considered unconscionable and spousal support would be awarded, regardless of what the cohabitation agreement said.

Note that if you are a high income earner and your partner is not, then you are going to need to be careful about limiting spousal support, particularly if your relationship lasts any length of time. Often the best you can do is minimize the amount of spousal support you will pay, rather than eliminate it entirely.

When you are deciding what to put into your agreement regarding spousal support, you need to think carefully about all of the vagaries of life. Simply because you and your partner are doing well financially now does not mean that will always be the case. In particular, you should consider: what happens if one of you becomes unemployed and unable to find a new job, what happens if you have children, what happens if one of you becomes disabled, what happens on retirement, what happens if one of you needs to give up a job to accommodate the other's career, and so on.

Spousal Support Options
Here are some options you can consider:

OPTION: Don't put anything in regarding spousal support
If you do not put anything in your cohabitation agreement regarding spousal support, the regular rules of spousal support will apply. This is a perfect option for the traditional younger couple who plan on having children together. Given that neither of you is likely to be established in your careers

yet, you will be having children, and you could be together a very long time, it can be difficult to predict what will happen in the future. Simply being silent on the issue is likely your best bet in these circumstances.

OPTION: Complete spousal support release
This option basically means that no matter what happens, no spousal support will ever be payable by either party. This may be appropriate in situations where a couple is older, does not plan to have children, and are established financially.

OPTION: Partial spousal support release
This option basically means that no spousal support is payable except in circumstances that are set out in the cohabitation agreement. Examples of these circumstances may be one party becoming disabled, or the couple having children.

OPTION: Low range of the Spousal Support Advisory Guidelines
As discussed earlier in this chapter, the Spousal Support Advisory Guidelines don't provide a single number for the amount of spousal support; instead they provide a range. The idea behind this option is that the low end of the range is chosen. The advantage of this is that it is flexible enough to accommodate pretty much whatever happens in the future. As well, it is very unlikely to be found unconscionable by a court, and thus invalid, as the amount of spousal support payable will be within the range set out by the Guidelines.

OPTION: Your own formula for spousal support
Don't like the amount set out in the Spousal Support Advisory Guidelines? You can create your own formula to deal with the uniqueness of your own situation. Many couples come to me with their own formula, often based on a percentage of what

the higher income earner earns, or a percentage of the difference between their two incomes.

OPTION: Fixed amount
You either pay a certain lump sum amount or a fixed amount each month if your relationship ends. In determining this amount, you should take inflation into account, and perhaps even index this amount to the Consumer Price Index. Also note that unlike monthly spousal support, lump sum spousal support is not tax deductible by the payor or taxable in the hands of the recipient.

OPTION: Different amounts based on the length of the relationship
A certain amount will be payable if the relationship is less than, for instance, two years, a higher amount will be payable if the relationship lasts, for example, from two to five years, and a higher amount still will be paid the longer the relationship is.

OPTION: Time limited
If you are not happy with how long spousal support is payable under the Spousal Support Advisory Guidelines, you can set out in your cohabitation agreement how long you agree that it should be payable.

OPTION: Specific purpose
You can limit spousal support in your cohabitation agreement so that it will only be paid for a specific purpose, for instance, so that one party can obtain a degree, or get retrained for a new job.

OPTION: No compensation for something
You can state in your cohabitation agreement that there will be no compensation for a particular choice made by a party. For

instance, if your partner gives up a job to move to your city when you get married, you can state that there will be no compensation for this.

OPTION: Disability insurance required
If your partner is disabled and unable to earn an income, spousal support payments are likely, regardless of what your cohabitation agreement says. One way to protect yourself against this is to require each partner to carry disability insurance.

OPTION: Income from certain sources not considered for spousal support
Perhaps you receive income from rental properties you own, or are the beneficiary of a trust when you get married. In this scenario, you may not want to pay spousal support based on these income streams, especially as they existed prior to relationship. A cohabitation agreement can exclude income sources from being considered in determining the amount of spousal support. In doing this, you need to be careful that you are not excluding so much that the spousal support provisions would be considered unconscionable by a court.

OPTION: Maximum income upon which spousal support is payable
If you are a high income earner, and your partner is not, and you play around with a spousal support calculator, you will see that the amounts of spousal support payable can be quite high. However, you can add a clause in your cohabitation agreement that basically sets a maximum income for the purposes of calculating spousal support. For instance, you can say that spousal support will be based on an annual income of $200,000 (likely adjusted for inflation) if your income is that much or higher. This will make sense particularly if the figure

chosen accurately represents the standard of living enjoyed during the relationship.

OPTION: Set out a formula for calculating your income
In all my discussions so far, I have assumed that it is easy to determine what a person's income is. That is true for a typical employee, who receives a T4 at the end of the year. However, if you own a business, to a certain extent you have control over your income in the sense that you determine how much to pay yourself, and whether to take an income or dividends. For family law purposes, this means that your entire business is fair game for investigation to see if there is income in there that can be considered income for family law purposes. This results in thousands of dollars in legal and accounting fees expended to determine what your income is. Setting out some parameters to limit the scope of this investigation may be possible. (It will not be all that helpful if you have children, as for determining child support, you will still need to go through this exercise).

Chapter 6: PROPERTY DIVISION

What is Property?
Under family law, property has a very extensive definition. Basically, it means not just real estate, but any and all assets, even including pensions, and includes assets acquired prior to your relationship, any increase in their value during your relationship, and any assets acquired after you began cohabiting.

What is the Law regarding Division of Property?
Under the Constitution, property is a provincial matter. So each province and territory has its own property division regime. A lot of the property division regimes are similar in their general principles; however, the details vary from province to province. I will go through what the situation is in each province shortly.

To complicate matters, in many provinces, property division for common law couples is different than for married couples.

The Traditional Rule for Common Law Couples
The traditional rule for common law couples is that when a couple separates, each person keeps what is in his or her own name. This means you keep your own bank accounts, pensions, RRSPs, vehicles, and so on, and so does your partner. It does not make a difference who paid for what, who did what, or where the money originally came from.

If property is in both your name and your partner's name, such as a home or a joint bank account, then that property is shared between the two of you. If you and your partner cannot agree on how to divide the assets, the court will normally order it sold and the proceeds shared.

Each person is responsible for the payment of their own debts.

This is still the rule in many provinces and territories for common law couples, and this is the most common regime that people choose to put into their cohabitation agreement.

In such a regime, for any asset that does not have title, you want to ensure that you keep the receipt to show that you own it. For instance, if you buy an expensive piece of art, you claim it is yours, and your partner claims it is theirs. How is a judge going to decide who is telling the truth? Having a receipt and showing the money coming from your bank account or credit card will normally be sufficient to succeed.

As well, in such a regime, you want to ensure that you are on title to anything to which you are contributing, financially or otherwise. Otherwise, your partner will benefit from all of your financial contributions and owe you nothing. I have lost track of the number of times someone has come to my office in tears stating that for years they have paid half the mortgage and utilities on the family home that is solely in their partner's name, and now their partner is kicking them out and not giving them anything.

Unjust Enrichment

Obviously, the traditional rule for the division of property for common law couples can be quite harsh. After a twenty-year relationship and several children together, one person could walk away with almost everything, and the other person could have almost nothing. In the circumstances, the courts looked for various ways to soften these results and make them fairer. So, they applied what is called the law of unjust enrichment.

What does this mean? If one partner is not happy with each person keeping their own assets and liabilities, they can claim a share of their partner's assets on the ground that their partner was unjustly enriched during the relationship. To do that, they must show three things:

1. <u>Enrichment</u> – one partner has been enriched due to his or her partner's effort, work, or financial contribution. A person's contribution may have been domestic services, such as housekeeping, child care, unpaid work in a partner's business, yard work, repairs or renovations, and may also include financial contributions, or quasi-financial contributions such as the purchase of consumables for the family. As a result of a person's efforts, has their partner improved their lot? The answer is often yes, if he or she has assets, or paid off debts, or improved his or her property. Almost anything done for a person's partner will have enriched him somehow.

2. <u>Deprivation</u> – the other partner has suffered deprivation, normally by sacrificing time, money, future prospects, and so on. This is usually the converse of the enrichment. A person will have put himself or herself out caring for their partner's interests and in the process will have sacrificed their own opportunities, energy, free time, future, and prospects. There is a presumption in a long-term relationship, in the absence of contrary evidence, that the enrichment of one partner has resulted in a deprivation of the other.

3. <u>No legal reason</u> – there was no legal obligation to provide the enrichment. If a person was under no contractual or statutory obligation to provide the contribution he or she did, then there is no legal reason for the enrichment. Again, this will normally be the case for an unmarried couple.

Here are some examples of cases where the court has found unjust enrichment:

<u>Pettkus v Becker</u> – Woman supported man for first 5 years of their common law relationship, so he could save to acquire a bee farm. The bee farm was purchased in his name. Woman then took a major role in running the bee farm. The Supreme Court of Canada decided that the man was unjustly enriched.

<u>Sorochan v Sorochan</u> – During a 42-year common law relationship, woman performed all of the domestic duties, raised the 6 children, and worked long hours on the farm. The Supreme Court of Canada decided that man was unjustly enriched.

<u>Peter v Beblow</u> – During a 12-year common law relationship, woman raised children from her previous relationship and from man's previous relationship. After the first year, she worked outside the home, contributing financially, although never as much as man. She also worked in and around the house, improving it, and gardening. The Supreme Court of Canada found that the man had been unjustly enriched.

Joint Family Venture

The courts have recently made it easier to succeed in a claim for unjust enrichment. In the past, you would need to show some sort of connection between the contribution you made, and the enrichment your partner made. Now, rather than showing a direct causal link, there is a concept that the family is functioning as a unit, and each partner is a partner in a joint family venture.

Quantum Meruit

Once you have established that one party has been unjustly enriched, the next question is what to do about it. If someone has contributed 10 hours of labour without compensation, calculating an appropriate remedy is fairly straightforward. You can figure out a reasonable hourly rate for that type of work, multiply it by 10, and then you have a ballpark figure. This is known as "quantum meruit" – an award of money to compensate for a contribution that has unjustly enriched someone else. You can do that in family law cases, but often that is difficult to calculate years after the fact, or the end result would be an astronomical amount of money.

Constructive Trust

What courts do in this sort of situation is award people what is known as a "constructive trust" interest in their partner's assets. Let's figure out what that means. The idea behind a trust is that one person has legal title to an asset, but he is to use that asset for the benefit of others. So, for instance, if someone dies and has minor children, they may leave their money to another adult to manage, but the funds are to be used to raise the children. This is an example of a trust.

However, the court can impose a trust on any asset – this is the "constructive" part – the court is constructing a trust where there was not one before. So the court could say something like your partner helped you advance your career, so you hold part of your assets in trust for them. So your assets would still be in your name, but it would be for the benefit of your partner. In essence, the court is saying that even though the asset is yours, part of it belongs to your partner.

Example
Let's look at the example I mentioned earlier of someone paying half the mortgage, utilities, taxes, and repair for a home that is not in their name.

Using the principles of unjust enrichment, a court would likely find:

Enrichment – the home owner is better off because these bills were paid by someone else.

Deprivation – the person who paid the bills is worse off because of paying all that and getting nothing in return.

No legal reason – the person who paid the bills had no obligation to do so.

Based on that, a court would likely find that there had been unjust enrichment.

What to do about that? In a short-term relationship, the person who paid all these bills could likely be refunded any contributions made, less rent that would have been paid. In a longer-term relationship, where the contributions have been going on for many years, and there may be other non-financial contributions as well, a court is likely to impose a constructive trust on the house, maybe even up to half of the house in a long enough relationship.

Wow, that is all very complicated!
Yes, and actually, I have really oversimplified it and glossed over a lot of things just to present it here. You can see how things can get messy and expensive really quickly in this situation. A court essentially needs to go through your entire relationship, and see who contributed what, often both financially and non-financially. This is a major reason why you should always get a cohabitation agreement – it allows you to avoid this difficult legal situation.

Executive Summary
I have simplified this greatly, but I know that this is still quite

complicated. It boils down to this. The basic rule is that each party keeps what is in his or her name. If you do not like that, you can get involved in a messy lawsuit known as a claim for unjust enrichment. The courts are over time making it easier to succeed in that kind of a lawsuit, and in longer relationships, particularly where there are children, the result is often close to what would happen if you were married. You do not want to go down that road if possible. A cohabitation agreement can protect you from having to go down this road.

Now that we have gone through the general principles, let us look at the specific legal situation for property division in each province and territory.

Ontario

In Ontario, a common law partner has no right to seek an equalization of net family property (the legal term for a division of assets). Each person keeps what is in his or her name. Jointly owned property is shared. Each person is responsible for his or her own debts. If one partner is not happy with the results that this brings, he or she can bring a claim for unjust enrichment (see earlier in this chapter for an explanation of how that works).

British Columbia

British Columbia provides a good example of why a cohabitation agreement is helpful. In the last three years, the legal situation relating to common law couples has changed dramatically. The rules relating to the division of property used to be similar to those in Ontario, where each party keeps what is in his or her name. Now common law couples who have lived together for two years or more are treated the same as married couples. (Even if you have a child together, you still must reach the two-year mark for the property division rules to apply).

In British Columbia, all "family property" is divided equally between the partners. Property excluded from family property includes property owned before relationship, inheritances, gifts from third parties, personal injury awards, proceeds of life insurance policies, and beneficial interests in discretionary trusts in certain cases. The increase in value of excluded property is included in family property.

If you have not yet lived together for two years, you can still bring a claim for unjust enrichment (see earlier in this chapter for an explanation of how that works).

Alberta

In Alberta, a common law partner has no right to seek a division of assets. Each person keeps what is in his or her name. Jointly owned property is shared. Each person is responsible for his or her own debts. If one partner is not happy with the results that this brings, he or she can bring a claim for unjust enrichment (see earlier in this chapter for an explanation of how that works).

Saskatchewan

In Saskatchewan, common law couples who have lived together for two years or more are treated the same as married couples. This means that all "family property" is divided equally. Property acquired before relationship is exempt, as well as personal injury awards, proceeds of life insurance policies, but not increases in their value during the relationship.

If you have not yet lived together for two years, you can still bring a claim for unjust enrichment (see earlier in this chapter for an explanation of how that works).

Manitoba

In Manitoba, common law couples who have lived in a

conjugal relationship for three years, or who have registered their relationship at the Vital Statistics Registry, are treated the same for property division as are married couples. This means that each partner values all their assets on the date of separation. The partner with the greater net worth then pays half the difference in net worth to the other partner. Jointly owned assets are not covered. Gifts and inheritances are exempt from division. Assets owned at the date of relationship are exempt from division, but any increase in their value is not.

If you have not yet lived together for three years, you can still bring a claim for unjust enrichment (see earlier in this chapter for an explanation of how that works).

Nova Scotia
In Nova Scotia, if you are living common law, you have a choice of going down two different roads. You can choose to formally register your relationship by filing a domestic partners declaration under the Vital Statistics Act. If you do that, you and your partner are considered domestic partners, and you have all the same rights regarding property division as you would have if you were married.

This means that if you are domestic partners, matrimonial property is divided equally between the partners. This includes all property except third-party gifts, inheritances, personal injury awards, proceeds of life insurance policies, personal items, and business assets.

If you do not formally register your relationship, you have no right to seek a division of assets. Each person keeps what is in his or her name. Jointly owned property is shared. Each person is responsible for his or her own debts. If one partner is not happy with the results that this brings, he or she can bring a claim for unjust enrichment (see earlier in this chapter for an explanation of how that works).

New Brunswick

In New Brunswick, a common law partner has no right to seek a division of assets. Each person keeps what is in his or her name. Jointly owned property is shared. Each person is responsible for his or her own debts. If one partner is not happy with the results that this brings, he or she can bring a claim for unjust enrichment (see earlier in this chapter for an explanation of how that works).

Newfoundland and Labrador

In Newfoundland and Labrador, a common law partner has no right to seek a division of assets. Each person keeps what is in his or her name. Jointly owned property is shared. Each person is responsible for his or her own debts. If one partner is not happy with the results that this brings, he or she can bring a claim for unjust enrichment (see earlier in this chapter for an explanation of how that works).

Prince Edward Island

In Prince Edward Island, a common law partner has no right to seek a division of assets. Each person keeps what is in his or her name. Jointly owned property is shared. Each person is responsible for his or her own debts. If one partner is not happy with the results that this brings, he or she can bring a claim for unjust enrichment (see earlier in this chapter for an explanation of how that works).

Northwest Territories

In Northwest Territories, if you and your partner have lived in a marriage-like relationship for two years or more, or if you and your partner have lived in a marriage-like relationship for less than two years and have a child together, then property division works the same way as if you were married.

The way that property division works in the Northwest Territories is as follows. The increase in value of assets of both parties during the marriage is shared, (with the exception of certain assets, discussed below). If you want to get into the nitty gritty of the calculation, add together the value of all of your assets, deduct from this value of all of your debts, deduct from this the value of all of your assets on the date of marriage, and add to this the value all of your debts on your date of marriage. This gives you your "net family property." Do the same for your spouse.

Then an "equalization payment" is made. The amount of the equalization payment is half the difference between your and your spouse's net family property. So, after the equalization payment, you should both have the same net family property. For instance, if your net family property is $100,000 and your spouse's net family property is $50,000, you would make an equalization payment of $25,000 to your spouse, so that you are each left with $75,000.

Note that it is the <u>value</u> of the assets that is divided, and not the assets themselves.

As mentioned earlier, certain assets are excluded from the calculation of your net family property, namely inheritances, gifts from third parties, proceeds of life insurance policies, and personal injury awards.

If you have not yet lived together long enough to qualify for an automatic property division, then you can still bring a claim for unjust enrichment (see earlier in this chapter for an explanation of how that works).

Yukon

In Yukon, a common law partner has no right to seek a division of assets. Each person keeps what is in his or her name. Jointly owned property is shared. Each person is responsible for his or her own debts. If one partner is not happy with the results that this brings, he or she can bring a claim for unjust enrichment (see earlier in this chapter for an explanation of how that works).

Nunavut

In Nunavut, if you and your partner have lived in a marriage-like relationship for two years or more, or if you and your partner have lived in a marriage-like relationship for less than two years and have a child together, then property division works the same way as if you were married.

The way that property division works in the Nunavut is as follows. The increase in value of assets of both parties during the marriage is shared, (with the exception of certain assets, discussed below). If you want to get into the nitty gritty of the calculation, add together the value of all of your assets, deduct from this value of all of your debts, deduct from this the value of all of your assets on the date of marriage, and add to this the value all of your debts on your date of marriage. This gives you your "net family property." Do the same for your spouse.

Then an "equalization payment" is made. The amount of the equalization payment is half the difference between your and your spouse's net family property. So, after the equalization payment, you should both have the same net family property. For instance, if your net family property is $100,000 and your spouse's net family property is $50,000, you would make an equalization payment of $25,000 to your spouse, so that you are each left with $75,000.

Note that it is the <u>value</u> of the assets that is divided, and not the assets themselves.

As mentioned earlier, certain assets are excluded from the calculation of your net family property, namely inheritances, gifts from third parties, proceeds of life insurance policies, and personal injury awards.

If you have not yet lived together long enough to qualify for an automatic property division, then you can still bring a claim for unjust enrichment (see earlier in this chapter for an explanation of how that works).

Property Division in a Cohabitation Agreement

For most people this is the heart of the cohabitation agreement. So long as you and your partner agree on it, you can put pretty much anything about property division that you want into a cohabitation agreement (so long as it is not unconscionable, or in British Columbia, significantly unfair). You can deal with currently owned assets, the increase in the value of these assets during your relationship, and any assets that are acquired during the relationship. You can deal with the home you and your partner live in (see the next chapter for more information about this). You can deal with business interests or pensions. You can be as creative as you want and tailor things to your situation as much as you want. Here are some typical scenarios I see in my practice.

Property Division Options

Here are some options you can consider:

OPTION: Separate as to property
This property regime is what most people think of when they think of a cohabitation agreement – what is mine is mine, and what is your is yours. Ownership is determined by title. If

something is jointly owned, it is shared between the parties. Throughout your relationship you can control exactly who gets what through title. For instance, if you want a cottage shared 60/40, simply ensure that the title states that one of you owns 60% of the cottage, and the other owns 40% of the cottage.

This property regime is essentially the traditional rule for common law couples. It works well for older couples who are already established financially, have good careers, and do not plan on having children. This property regime also works well for second and subsequent relationships, where the couple wants to preserve their assets for their children from a previous relationship.

OPTION: Certain assets not divided
Under this option, a couple will divide their assets as if they were a married couple. However, they exclude some assets from this division of property, for instance, a home, a pension, a family farm, or a business. This is the option most people are thinking of when they say "I want to protect my 'xyz' in a cohabitation agreement."

In choosing this option, you need to consider the future of the asset in question. For something like a government pension, excluding it from division is straightforward, as the pension is governed by certain rules and there is normally not much a person can do to manipulate this.

However, for instance, what if the excluded asset is a family home, and you need to move to a new home. What if the new home costs substantially more than the excluded home? Or costs substantially less? If the excluded asset is a business, what is to stop the business owner from not taking out any money from the business, or from putting all of their savings into the business? This does not make excluding those assets wrong – it just means you need to think about all future possibilities and deal with them in your cohabitation agreement.

OPTION: Property divided as in another jurisdiction

I see this option chosen a lot by immigrants. For instance, the couple comes from Germany, and wants their property treated as it would be if they were governed by German family law. But you do not need to be an immigrant to benefit from this option. Common law couples are treated differently in each province in Canada, and the treatment of common law couples in one province may be more appealing to you then in your home province.

OPTION: Property divided as set out in your current provincial regime

Even if you are happy with how property is divided under your current provincial laws, these rules can change over time, or you may move to another province, both of which can dramatically affect your legal rights. You can crystallize the current property division scheme in your province by using a cohabitation agreement.

OPTION: Protect inheritances and gifts

Say that you will be receiving $100,000 from your parents, and want to use that money to buy a matrimonial home. In many provinces, if you did not buy the home, this money would not be subject to property division, but by buying a matrimonial home, it is. A cohabitation agreement can ensure that even if you put inheritances or gifts from third parties into a home, or commingle your inheritances or gifts with family assets, those funds will not be subject to property division.

OPTION: Protect yourself from your partner's debts

Your partner is not the best at managing money, and routinely runs up large debts. Even without a cohabitation agreement, you will not be directly responsible for these debts. However, in provinces and territories where common law couples are treated like married couples, this can dramatically affect how property division works. A cohabitation agreement can exclude certain debts from being used in calculating the division of property.

OPTION: Dealing with a business
If only one partner owns a business, and the other one is not involved in the business, then you can deal with the business as you would any other asset. However, if you and your partner are both involved in the business, particularly if both of you have an ownership interest, then your cohabitation agreement should set out what happens to the business if your relationship ends, ideally providing a mechanism for one partner to buy the other partner out.

OPTION: Treat property as if you were married
You do not want to get married, but you do like the clean way that all property accumulated during the marriage is shared equally by the couple. In that case, your cohabitation agreement can set out that your property will be divided as if you were married. (As discussed above, some provinces and territories treat common law couples the same as if they were unmarried, some do not after a certain period of time).

OPTION: No unjust enrichment
Earlier in the chapter I discussed what unjust enrichment is, and how it is a complex and costly legal claim. If you and your partner have agreed on a property division regime to put into your cohabitation agreement, then a claim for unjust enrichment would essentially be an attempt to do an end run around the cohabitation agreement. Every cohabitation

agreement I have ever drafted or seen prohibits a claim for unjust enrichment.

OPTION: Set out date of relationship assets

This option is useful in provinces and territories where common law couples are treated the same as married couples. In those jurisdictions, the treatment of assets owned at the date you started cohabiting is different than from assets acquired after that date. You can use a cohabitation agreement to set out your and your partner's assets. The reality is if your relationship lasts 10 or 20 years, it can be difficult to recall exactly what you owned when your relationship began, much less come up with documentary proof for it. Many separations involve people squabbling about what they brought into the relationship. This sort of a provision ensures that you really get credit for what you owned when your relationship began, regardless of how much time has passed, how much memories fade, and how difficult it is to locate bank statements from years ago.

Chapter 7: MATRIMONIAL HOME

What is a Matrimonial Home?

The matrimonial home is the home you and your partner live in. Often, this is a couple's most valuable asset and it is often dealt with separately in a cohabitation agreement, as people want it to be treated differently than other assets.

There can be more than one matrimonial home. For instance, if you and your partner live in one home for the winter and another home for the summer, both may be matrimonial homes. Or, if you spend most of your time living in a home, and your partner spends most of their time living in the cottage, both the home and the cottage may be matrimonial homes.

What is the Law regarding Matrimonial Homes?

Many provinces give matrimonial homes special treatment under the law. The idea is that a home is a special kind of asset, with more than just monetary value, as it is where you, your partner, and perhaps your children, live.

To complicate matters further, just like property division, the treatment of the matrimonial home is different in each province.

Additionally, some provinces treat matrimonial homes differently for married couples than for unmarried couples. As discussed at the beginning of this book, if you and your partner get married, your cohabitation agreement becomes a prenuptial agreement.

While normally that is not an issue, when it comes to the matrimonial home it may be. Some provinces and territories do not permit people to give up rights other than ownership rights to a matrimonial home in a prenuptial agreement, and if you have these sorts of provisions in your cohabitation agreement, they will become invalid upon marriage.

To give a concrete example, say that you have a clause in your cohabitation agreement stating that within 90 days of your relationship ending, one partner will move out of the home. While that sort of clause is fine to put into a cohabitation agreement, in Ontario, that clause would become invalid upon marriage. A married couple in Ontario is not allowed to agree in advance who will leave the matrimonial home when their relationship ends, regardless of who owns the home.

Note that normally, only the particular clause relating to the matrimonial home becomes invalid – not the entire cohabitation agreement.

Matrimonial Home Rights

Generally, when people think of an asset, they think about one particular legal right – ownership. For instance, who owns the home?

However, with a matrimonial home, there are three additional rights that you should be aware of.

Possession – Possession means the right to live in the home, regardless of ownership. If you do not have possessory rights, and you do not own part of your home, then your partner can simply kick you out and change the locks to the home. Some provinces and territories provide possessory rights to common law partners, some do not.

Disposition – Disposition means the right to sell the home. In some provinces and territories, the owner of the home may need the permission of his or her common law partner to sell the home, even if the partner has no ownership interest. In other jurisdictions, this is not necessary. Note the similarity of this right to possession. Selling the home to someone else can essentially have the same effect as kicking your partner out, as in both cases your partner needs to leave the home.

Encumbrance – Encumbrance means the right to mortgage the home. Again, in some provinces and territories, the owner of the home may need the permission of his or her common law partner to mortgage the home, even if the partner has no ownership interest. In other jurisdictions, this is not necessary. Note the similarity of this right to that of disposition. Encumbering the home so that there is no equity left in the home is similar in effect to selling the home. A person can simply strip all the equity from the home, then not make payments, and have the financial institution foreclose on the home. Alternatively, a person can mortgage the home to a friend, have the friend foreclose, essentially resulting in a sale of the home to the friend.

In crafting a cohabitation agreement, you will want to think carefully about the matrimonial home, and not just its ownership. Each province has different rules for the ownership and division of matrimonial homes, as well as for their possession, disposition and encumbrance.

Ontario
In Ontario, for common law couples, there are no special rules regarding a matrimonial home. You can put whatever you want in your cohabitation agreement regarding the matrimonial home.

British Columbia
In British Columbia, the matrimonial home is known as the family residence. Once you and your partner have lived

together for two years, you have the same rights regarding the family residence as if you were married. This means that one partner cannot kick the other out of the residence, nor can one partner sell or mortgage the residence without the other partner's permission. There are no special rules in British Columbia regarding the division of the family residence; it is treated like any other family property. If you and your partner have not lived together for two years, then there are no special rights that apply to the family residence.

Alberta

In Alberta, for common law couples, there are no special rules regarding a matrimonial home, known as homestead. You can put whatever you want in your cohabitation agreement regarding the homestead.

Saskatchewan

In Saskatchewan, common law couples who have lived together for two years or more are treated the same as married couples, which means that the matrimonial home, known in Saskatchewan as the family home, is treated differently than other property. Prior to the two-year mark, there are no special rules regarding a family home in Saskatchewan.

In Saskatchewan, the equity in a family home, or the value of that equity, is normally divided equally. Normally property acquired before a relationship starts is exempt from division – this does not normally apply to the family home. So, if you bring an asset into the relationship, say $100,000 in cash, then when you separate, you get credit for bringing that asset into the relationship. However, if that same $100,000 was instead $100,000 of equity in a family home, and you are still living in that same home on the date of separation, you would NOT normally get credit for bringing that asset into the relationship. So, in both cases, you are entering into the relationship with the same amount of money, but in one case, because the money was invested in a home, you get a substantially worse result on separation.

Manitoba

In Manitoba, common law couples who have lived in a conjugal relationship for three years, or who have registered their relationship at the Vital Statistics Registry, have their matrimonial home, known as homestead, treated in the same way as married couples. This means that one partner cannot kick the other out of the homestead, nor can one partner sell or mortgage the homestead without the other partner's permission. Prior to the three-year mark, there are no special rules regarding a homestead in Manitoba.

Nova Scotia

In Nova Scotia, if you are living common law, you have a choice of going down two different roads. You can choose to formally register your relationship by filing a domestic partners declaration under the Vital Statistics Act. If you do that, you and your partner are considered domestic partners, and you have all the same rights regarding a matrimonial home as you would have if you were married.

This means that one partner cannot kick the other out of the matrimonial home, nor can one partner sell or mortgage the matrimonial home without the other partner's permission. There are no special rules in Nova Scotia regarding the division of the matrimonial home; it is treated like any other family property.

If you do not formally register your relationship, there are no special rules regarding a matrimonial home. You can put whatever you want in your cohabitation agreement regarding the matrimonial home.

New Brunswick
In New Brunswick, for common law couples, there are no special rules regarding a matrimonial home, known as a marital home. You can put whatever you want in your cohabitation agreement regarding the marital home.

Newfoundland and Labrador
In Newfoundland and Labrador, for common law couples, there are no special rules regarding a matrimonial home. You can put whatever you want in your cohabitation agreement regarding the matrimonial home.

Prince Edward Island
In Prince Edward Island, for common law couples, there are no special rules regarding a matrimonial home, known as a family home. You can put whatever you want in your cohabitation agreement regarding the family home.

Northwest Territories
In Northwest Territories, if you and your partner have lived in a marriage-like relationship for two years or more, or if you and your partner have lived in a marriage-like relationship for less than two years and have a child together, then the family home is treated as if you were married. This means that one partner cannot kick the other out of the family home, nor can one partner sell or mortgage the family home without the other partner's permission. Prior to the two-year mark, there are no special rules regarding a family home in Northwest Territories.

Yukon
In Yukon, for common law couples, there are no special rules regarding a matrimonial home. You can put whatever you

want in your cohabitation agreement regarding the matrimonial home.

Nunavut

In Nunavut, if you and your partner have lived in a marriage-like relationship for two years or more, or if you and your partner have lived in a marriage-like relationship for less than two years and have a child together, then the family home is treated as if you were married. This means that one partner cannot kick the other out of the family home, nor can one partner sell or mortgage the family home without the other partner's permission. Prior to the two-year mark, there are no special rules regarding a family home in Nunavut.

Matrimonial Homes in a Cohabitation Agreement

A lot of people come to me with the impression that they cannot deal with the matrimonial home in a cohabitation agreement. This is not the case. A lot of people enter into cohabitation agreement just to deal with their homes, as that is their major asset.

Note that you can deal with a future matrimonial home in your cohabitation agreement - you need not even own one at the time you enter into your cohabitation agreement. You can plan out in advance how you and your partner will deal with the purchase of a home to live in when the time comes.

Matrimonial Home Options

In a cohabitation agreement, you can treat your matrimonial home the same as all of your other assets, or you can single it out and treat it differently. You can be as creative as you want in your treatment of the home, as long as both you and your partner agree and find the treatment fair. To get you started, here are some typical types of arrangements I've seen:

OPTION: Matrimonial home always belongs to one party
One common way people deal with matrimonial homes in their cohabitation agreements is to state that no matter what happens, the matrimonial home will always belong to the owner. In other words, it is completely excluded from any division of property. Many people have worked hard their entire lives so that they can own a home; they don't want to lose half of it if their relationship goes south.

Note that, as discussed earlier in this book, just because you own the matrimonial home, does not mean you can kick your partner out, or that you can sell, transfer, rent, or mortgage your home. In some provinces and territories you will be able to do so; in others, you won't.

In choosing this option, you need to consider what happens if you move in the future. Does this provision apply only to the home existing at the time your relationship started, or does it also apply to future homes? What if your future home costs substantially more or less than your current home? You are permitted to deal with a currently existing home in a different way than a home that may be purchased in the future.

OPTION: Interest in home obtained through relationship
The idea here is that the longer the relationship, the larger the interest that the originally non-owning partner gets. A typical example of this is one partner obtaining a 2% interest in the home for each year of relationship, until a maximum of 50% is reached. This sort of arrangement is common where one partner does not work and will not be able to contribute financially to the home.

OPTION: Each partner gets a certain percentage of the home
Perhaps one partner paid for 2/3 of the home and the other paid for 1/3 of the home. They are sharing expenses related to

the upkeep of the home 2/3 and 1/3. Then the home is divided 2/3 and 1/3.

OPTION: Each partner gets their down payment back; the rest of the equity in the home is shared equally

This seems to be a very popular option. Typically, one of the first things couples do when they move in together is to buy a home together. In doing so, they want to maximize the down payment that they make, yet each of them may be able to contribute a different amount. For instance, one partner may put in $60,000 towards the purchase of the home, and the other partner may put in $30,000 towards the purchase of the home. In this case, the couple agrees that when the home is divided or sold, the first partner gets the $60,000 back, and other partner gets the $30,000 back, and the remaining equity in the home is shared equally between them.

OPTION: One partner gets credit for all contributions made to home

In this situation, one partner owns the home, but sometimes the other will make financial contributions to the home. The cohabitation agreement requires that these contributions are kept track of, and reimbursed (sometimes with interest) when the home is sold or the relationship ends.

OPTION: House divided according to contributions

If you and your partner are scrupulous about keeping records, then you can agree to share the matrimonial home according to how much money each party has contributed. Basically, each of you would be reimbursed for any contributions made, and any increase in the home's equity would be shared.

OPTION: Possession, disposition, and encumbrance of home

While you may be fine with your partner owning the home you live in, regardless of what future financial circumstances are, as discussed earlier in this chapter, this can leave you in a very vulnerable position. In some provinces and territories, this can mean that you can be kicked out of the home, or find the home sold or foreclosed from under your feet. You may wish to include clauses in your cohabitation agreement that prohibit this.

OPTION: Setting out the mechanics of dividing the home
It is great that you and your partner agree who owns how much of the home. But if your relationship ends, that does not mean much, particularly when one of you decides to move out of the home. In a cohabitation agreement, you can set out the mechanics of dividing the home.

To do this, think about who will buy out the other party. For instance, it can be specified that one of you will buy the other out. Or the highest bidder will buy the other one out. Or one person will have an option to buy the other out, and if he or she declines, then the other person has the option to buy.

Think about valuation of the home. What will you do if you and your partner cannot agree on a value for the home to buy out the other. For instance, you can bid against each other for the home, or have a property appraisal done.

Think about timelines – how quickly do you want to deal with these issues.

Think about moving out – who will move out of the home and by when.

OPTION: Payment of housing expenses
Including something about payment of the mortgage, property taxes, and repairs can be important, particularly where the home belongs to only one party. As well, perhaps the owner of

the home will be charging the other partner the equivalent of rent for the home.

Chapter 8: ESTATES

Estates and Cohabitation

A cohabitation agreement comes into effect when your relationship ends. One way your relationship can end is by you or your partner passing away. Due to this, you can deal with estate law issues in your cohabitation agreement, albeit in a limited way. However, a cohabitation agreement cannot be a replacement for a will.

What is the Law regarding Estates?

No Will

If you pass away without a will, that is known in legal jargon as passing away "intestate." There are specific rules about what happens to a person's property if he or she passes away intestate. Under the Constitution, property is a provincial matter, so each province and territory has its own rules. To complicate matters, the intestacy rules are often different for unmarried and married couples. The intestacy rules for each province and territory, for common law partners, are as follows.

Ontario

If your common law partner passes away without a will, for legal purposes, in Ontario you are strangers and you would not receive anything from their estate.

British Columbia

In British Columbia, if you and your partner have cohabited for two years or more, and you don't have a will, and there are no children, then your partner inherits everything.

If you and your partner have cohabited for two years or more, and you don't have a will, and there are children, then your partner gets the first $300,000 of your estate, and the remainder of your estate is split equally between your partner and your children.

For example, if you pass away intestate, have cohabited for more than two years, have two children and your estate is worth $600,000, the first $300,000 goes to your partner, and of the remaining $300,000, $100,000 goes to your partner, $100,000 goes to your first child, and $100,000 goes to you second child.

If you and your partner have not cohabited for two years or more, and one of you passes away without a will, the other would receive nothing from the estate of the deceased.

Alberta
In Alberta, if you and your partner have lived together in a relationship of interdependence for three years, or if you and your partner have lived together in a relationship of interdependence for less than three years, but the relationship is of some permanence, and there is a child of the relationship, or if you and your partner enter into an Adult Interdependent Partner Agreement, then you have the same estate law rights as if you were married.

This means that if there are no children, and one of you passes away without a will, the other inherits everything.

If you have children but no will, then your partner gets the first $150,000 of your estate, and the remainder of your estate is split equally between your partner and your children.

For example, if you pass away intestate, have two children and your estate is worth $450,000, the first $150,000 goes to your partner, and of the remaining $300,000, $100,000 goes to your partner, $100,000 goes to your first child, and $100,000 goes to you second child.

However, if you and your partner have NOT lived together in a relationship of interdependence for three years, or if you and your partner have NOT lived together in a relationship of interdependence for less than three years, but the relationship is of some permanence, and there is a child of the relationship, or if you and your partner have not entered into an Adult Interdependent Partner Agreement, and one of you passes away without a will, the other would receive nothing from the estate of the deceased.

Saskatchewan

In all provinces when you get married, your will is automatically invalidated. The thinking behind this is that the will was made before you had the chance to think about your new spouse, and you'd likely want to give your new spouse some or all of your estate.

Saskatchewan takes this one step further. After living together for two years, you become common law partners, and your will is automatically invalidated. So, as you approach the second anniversary of living together, you should consider getting a new will drafted. Similarly, if you move to Saskatchewan and have been in a common law relationship for more than two years, your will is automatically invalidated.

Common law and married partners have the same legal rights and obligations when it comes to estates in Saskatchewan.

This means that if there are no children, and one of you passes away without a will, the other inherits everything.

If you have children but no will, then your partner gets the first $100,000 of your estate, and the remainder of your estate is split equally between your partner and your children.

For example, if you pass away intestate, have two children and your estate is worth $400,000, the first $100,000 goes to your partner, and of the remaining $300,000, $100,000 goes to your partner, $100,000 goes to your first child, and $100,000 goes to you second child.

If you and your partner have not cohabited for two years or more, and one of you passes away without a will, the other would receive nothing from the estate of the deceased.

Manitoba

In Manitoba, if you and your partner have lived together in a conjugal relationship for three years, or if you and your partner have lived in a conjugal relationship for one year and are raising a child together, or if you and your partner have registered your relationship under the Vital Statistics Act, then you will be treated the same for estate law purposes as a married couple.

This means that if one of you passes away without a will, the other inherits everything, even if you have children together.

If you and your partner have NOT lived together in a conjugal relationship for three years, or if you and your partner have NOT lived in a conjugal relationship for one year and are raising a child together, or if you and your partner have NOT registered your relationship under the Vital Statistics Act, then if one of you passes away without a will, the other would receive nothing from the estate of the deceased.

Nova Scotia

In Nova Scotia, if you are living common law, you have a

choice of going down two different roads. You can choose to formally register your relationship by filing a domestic partners declaration under the Vital Statistics Act. If you do that, you and your partner are considered domestic partners, and you have all the same estate rights regarding as you would have if you were married.

This means that if there are no children, and one of you passes away without a will, the other inherits everything.

If you have children but no will, then your partner gets the first $50,000 of your estate, and the remainder of your estate is split equally between your partner and your children.

For example, if you pass away intestate, have two children and your estate is worth $350,000, the first $50,000 goes to your partner, and of the remaining $300,000, $100,000 goes to your partner, $100,000 goes to your first child, and $100,000 goes to you second child.

Alternatively, instead of getting the amount set out above, your partner instead elect to keep the matrimonial home instead of taking their preferential share, or if the home is worth less than the preferential share, a partner can elect to keep the matrimonial home as part of their preferential share. So, in the example above, if your equity in the matrimonial home was $250,000, then your spouse would get that, and the remaining $100,000 would be shared equally between your spouse and each child.

If you do not formally register your relationship, then if one of you passes away without a will, the other would receive nothing from the estate of the deceased.

New Brunswick
If your common law partner passes away without a will, for

legal purposes, in New Brunswick you are strangers and you would not receive anything from their estate.

Newfoundland and Labrador
If your common law partner passes away without a will, for legal purposes, in Newfoundland and Labrador you are strangers and you would not receive anything from their estate.

Prince Edward Island
If your common law partner passes away without a will, for legal purposes, in Newfoundland and Labrador you are strangers and you would not receive anything from their estate.

Northwest Territories
In Northwest Territories, if you and your partner have lived in a marriage-like relationship for two years or more, or if you and your partner have lived in a marriage-like relationship for less than two years and have a child together, then estate laws works the same way as if you were married.

This means that if there are no children, and one of you passes away without a will, the other inherits everything.

If you have children but no will, then your partner gets the first $50,000 of your estate, and the remainder of your estate is split equally between your partner and your children.

For example, if you pass away intestate, have two children and your estate is worth $350,000, the first $50,000 goes to your partner, and of the remaining $300,000, $100,000 goes to your partner, $100,000 goes to your first child, and $100,000 goes to you second child.

Alternatively, instead of getting the amount set out above, your partner instead elect to keep the matrimonial home instead of taking their preferential share, or if the home is worth less than the preferential share, a partner can elect to keep the matrimonial home as part of their preferential share. So, in the example above, if your equity in the matrimonial home was $250,000, then your spouse would get that, and the remaining $100,000 would be shared equally between your spouse and each child.

If you and your partner have NOT lived in a marriage-like relationship for two years or more, or if you and your partner have NOT lived in a marriage-like relationship for less than two years and have a child together, then if one of you passes away without a will, the other would receive nothing from the estate of the deceased.

Yukon

If your common law partner passes away without a will, for legal purposes, in Yukon you are strangers and you would not receive anything from their estate.

Nunavut

In Northwest Territories, if you and your partner have lived in a marriage-like relationship for two years or more, or if you and your partner have lived in a marriage-like relationship for less than two years and have a child together, then estate laws works the same way as if you were married.

This means that if there are no children, and one of you passes away without a will, the other inherits everything.

If you have children but no will, then your partner gets the first $50,000 of your estate, and the remainder of your estate is split equally between your partner and your children.

For example, if you pass away intestate, have two children and your estate is worth $350,000, the first $50,000 goes to your partner, and of the remaining $300,000, $100,000 goes to your partner, $100,000 goes to your first child, and $100,000 goes to you second child.

Alternatively, instead of getting the amount set out above, your partner instead elect to keep the matrimonial home instead of taking their preferential share, or if the home is worth less than the preferential share, a partner can elect to keep the matrimonial home as part of their preferential share. So, in the example above, if your equity in the matrimonial home was $250,000, then your spouse would get that, and the remaining $100,000 would be shared equally between your spouse and each child.

If you and your partner have NOT lived in a marriage-like relationship for two years or more, or if you and your partner have NOT lived in a marriage-like relationship for less than two years and have a child together, then if one of you passes away without a will, the other would receive nothing from the estate of the deceased.

But wait...
That's not all! Whether you pass away intestate or leave a will, your partner may have an option to make a matrimonial claim on your estate. The idea behind this is that you cannot simply cut your partner and children out of your inheritance through a will.

In Alberta, Saskatchewan, Manitoba, Northwest Territories, Nunavut and for domestic partners in Nova Scotia, there is legislation setting out minimum amounts of property that your partner must receive from your estate. In these provinces and territories, the surviving partner can elect to receive the same amount that he or she would have received if the two of you had separated on the day the other partner passed away. This normally amounts to half of all property that the two of you accumulate during the length of your relationship. Of course, you are not around to prove what you brought into the relationship, so although you normally would get credit for that, it may not happen in an estate law situation.

There's more...

Your partner may also be entitled to receive what is known as dependant's relief. The idea behind this is similar to spousal support – it is support so that your partner can continue to support himself or herself adequately. So even if you pass away without a will in a jurisdiction where common law partners have no estate rights, or you disinherit your common law partner, your common law partner may still be able to ask for money from your estate in the form of dependant's relief.

Estates in a Cohabitation Agreement

Many people choose not to deal with estate law issues in their cohabitation agreement, and that is a good approach, particularly if you are a younger couple, or if you are not sure how you want your estate handled.

There are typically two ways in which estate law issues are dealt with in a cohabitation agreement. In some provinces and territories, a common law partner has rights to your estate – either to receive a certain minimum amount from your estate, or to receive what could be considered the equivalent of spousal support from your estate. A cohabitation agreement can be used to release you and your partner from these rights. This is particularly the case where both of you may have children from a previous relationship, and want to leave your assets to your children.

The second way estate law issues are typically dealt with in a cohabitation agreement is to ensure minimum requirements for each other's will. For instance, in many provinces and territories, common law partners are legal strangers, and have no estate law rights. This means that a person may be able to disinherit a common law partner without consequence. You may wish to ensure that does not happen in your case, for instance by requiring each partner to leave their entire estate, or a portion of it, to the other. Or, you may wish to require your partner to allow you to live in the matrimonial home for a certain time period after your partner passes away, or even for the rest of your life.

Even if you deal with estate law issues in a cohabitation agreement, this does not preclude the necessity of having a will. It is a good idea to make a new will when you are about to get married, even in provinces where this is not required. Creating a new will is often done in conjunction with a creating a cohabitation agreement, as there is an overlap between the issues dealt with in each legal document.

Estate Law Options

Like property division, you can put pretty much anything into your cohabitation agreement about what will happen to your estate, so long as you and your partner agree to it.

Option: Do nothing

If you do not put anything in your cohabitation agreement about your estate, then all the regular rules regarding estates apply. This is a good option if you and your partner are entering a traditional first relationship, or even if you and your partner are not sure what you want to do with your estate.

Generally, people are willing to be more generous to their partner if their partner has stayed with them until they passed away, then if the relationship ends in a separation. So, this option is often a good one.

Option: Complete release
This means that neither you nor your partner are required to leave each other anything or support the other after one of you passes away. This is appropriate for older, financially established couples, particularly if one or both of them have children from a previous relationship.

Option: Minimum requirements
Your cohabitation agreement can require that you and your partner each leave the other a certain minimum amount of money or other assets. This guarantees a certain standard of living for the surviving partner, yet allows you more flexibility in dealing with your remaining assets.

Option: No matrimonial claim
As discussed above, legislation in some provinces and territories gives your partner an option to make a matrimonial claim against your assets, normally for the amount that they would inherit if you had separated on the day you passed away. This can be waived in a cohabitation agreement, allowing you more flexibility in determining how to plan your estate.

Option: Matrimonial home
A house is often a couple's main asset. You may wish to require that your partner leaves you the house if he or she passes away, or at least lets you stay there for the rest of your life.

Option: Life insurance
Often people have life insurance through employment that is a certain multiple of their annual income, or they may own other life insurance policies. A cohabitation agreement can require

that these policies designate the other partner as the beneficiary. A cohabitation agreement can even require a partner to obtain a policy for your benefit.

Option: Pensions
Often pensions have survivor benefits. Like life insurance, a cohabitation agreement can require that your partner designate you as the beneficiary of the pension survivor benefits.

Chapter 9: JURISDICTIONAL ISSUES

What is Jurisdiction?
In legal terms, jurisdiction refers to a geographic area and the law that applies in that area. So, Ontario is a jurisdiction, and Ontario law applies within that jurisdiction.

What is the Law regarding Jurisdiction?
The court where the defendant resides has jurisdiction over the defendant (the defendant is the person being sued). The court where property is located has jurisdiction over that property. The court where the children are living will have jurisdiction over issues relating to the children.

Normally, it will be obvious which jurisdiction to proceed in – it is where you and your partner are living. So, if you lived together in Vancouver, and separate there, then British Columbia is the appropriate jurisdiction, and the law of British Columbia applies.

Citizenship or nationality of a partner has no bearing on family law jurisdiction in Canada.

Jurisdiction in a Cohabitation Agreement
If you and your partner live in a particular province, and plan to spend the rest of your lives in that province, then jurisdiction is not an issue for you, and you can skip this chapter. However, nowadays people are more mobile, so the issue of jurisdiction is important.

If you and your partner live in different provinces, you will want to get a cohabitation agreement prepared in the province that you are going to be living in when you marry. For example, if you live in Toronto, and your partner lives in Vancouver, and when you marry your partner will join you in Toronto, you will want to get an Ontario cohabitation agreement.

If you have a cohabitation agreement in one province, and end up moving to another province (other than possibly Quebec; the law there is very different and you would need to consult with a Quebec lawyer), that will normally be fine. An Alberta court will normally uphold a Saskatchewan cohabitation agreement, and apply Saskatchewan law to its interpretation.

Cohabitation agreements become problematic, however, if you end up living in a jurisdiction outside of Canada. There is no guarantee that a foreign court, for instance a Florida or an English court, will uphold your agreement, regardless of what you put in your agreement. (Similarly, Canadian courts often do not uphold foreign cohabitation agreements). The reason for this is that family law differs dramatically from country to country, and the chances that a cohabitation agreement in one country will meet the requirements of a cohabitation agreement in another country are slim (in fact, many countries do not even recognize cohabitation agreements from their own jurisdiction). This is so even if you have a clause in your agreement stating that it is to be interpreted, for example, under Ontario law by an Ontario court.

If you know that it is very likely that you will be living in another country during your relationship, or even if it is a strong possibility that one partner would move to another country if your relationship ended, you should investigate entering into a cohabitation agreement in that other country as well. This would be a "mirror" cohabitation agreement – the same as your Canadian cohabitation agreement, but valid under the law of the foreign jurisdiction. You will need to work closely with lawyers in both jurisdictions to ensure that both cohabitation agreements are valid, and that one cohabitation agreement does not invalidate the other.

CONCLUSION

One thing that most people do not realize is that a cohabitation agreement does not need to be forever. You can set a time limit in the agreement after which the agreement, or part of it, expires.

Cohabitation agreements can also be flexible. Provided that you and your partner agree on a change, you and your partner can change a cohabitation agreement at any time, or even cancel the agreement altogether.

There is also something known as a review clause that you can include in a cohabitation agreement. Basically this clause states that after a certain number of years, say five or ten years, you and your partner will review what is in the agreement to determine whether it still makes sense. If it does not, then the two of you will decide how the agreement should be amended.

These are the basics of cohabitation agreements in Canada. If, after reading this book, you still have any questions about these agreements, I am always happy to hear from you. You can reach me via email through my website at CohabitationAgreement.ca.

DISCLAIMER

This book provides information about the law designed to help readers better understand the legal issues surrounding cohabitation agreements in Canada. But legal information is not the same as legal advice — the application of law to an individual's specific circumstances. Although I am a lawyer, and have done my best to ensure that this information is accurate and useful, you must consult a lawyer if you want professional assurance that this information, and your interpretation of it, is accurate. To clarify further, you may not rely upon this information as legal advice, nor as a recommendation or endorsement of any particular legal understanding.

Copyright 2016 by Jeffrey A Behrendt, BA, JD, LLM

www.ingramcontent.com/pod-product-compliance
Lightning Source LLC
Chambersburg PA
CBHW070106210526
45170CB00013B/768